REBEL

BREAKING FREE FROM RELIGION TO FIND GOD

ISBN: 978-0-578-64564-3

TABLE OF CONTENTS

Chapter 1

YOU HAVE NOT REBELLED ENOUGH.

"WHEN EVERYONE THINKS THE SAME, MAYBE NO ONE IS THINKING." - MATT BROWN

I had to stop, take a breath, and make a choice between my personal convictions and my future career. It wouldn't be the last time, but it was the first time and I felt sort of irrational. My entire education was leading up to a degree in counseling and psychology, I just had to prove one thing – that *I* wasn't crazy. It's kind of a prerequisite if you want help people be less crazy that you are not a psychopath yourself. That's frowned upon. And there is actually a test for this called the MMPI, a 500 question, true-false test designed to expose how insane you might be. Questions like, "*I like to hurt animals.*" "*I like to start fires.*" Nope. I just kept repeating to myself, "*Don't be crazy. Don't be crazy. Don't be crazy...*"

About halfway through the test I'm feeling good. I'm not a pyro or the next James Bond super villain. Then I get to this question.

"I believe in ghosts, Bigfoot, the Tooth Fairy or angels."

I read it again slowly and my heart sank. This question was put in here for people like me – Christians. Generally, my counseling community did not believe in God. They could not imagine that healthy, rational people actually hold the belief there is a creator out there. It sounds like a fairy tale, I get it. So this MMPI, in a not-so-subtle way, dismisses a spiritual world including... you guessed it, angels. Why are angels listed along with the Tooth Fairy? Because to believe in either one, I must be crazy or four years old, right?

As I sat there thinking about scratching off the other three choices, or leaving some not-so-Jesus-like comments in the margin, I realized it wasn't going to change their mind. I scanned down and two questions later was another jab, *"I hear voices in my head, or I believe God speaks to me."* You're kidding me! Yes, I believe God speaks to people too. Not in the kooky way they imagine but still. At this point I literally looked to see if there were cameras hidden somewhere thinking, *"Am I being Punk'd?"*

I was screwed if I answered truthfully, but I didn't have a choice in my heart to do anything else. I began to feel a little irritated that I was forced to face this kind of faith-scrubbing hurdle. But it's currently the status quo to reject the idea of a real, living God who loves us. So that day was the end of my counseling career, but another marker in the story of rebellion in my life. A rebellion against the mainstream, where everyone assumes God is a joke.

I experienced what's it feels like to be a rebel growing up involved with action sports. Before I could drive, I was traveling the country competing in events with my BMX and skater friends, but coming home to a small town where no one knew, understood or really cared. The entire action sports community was seen as a deviant, irresponsible gang of troublemakers and this profiling often landed on me in a negative way. Most of my friends share some of the same sketchy experiences of being kicked out of places, threatened with fines, yelled at by strangers, or robbed of their bikes or gear. There were plenty of times I felt like the world around me was saying, "*You don't think, act, dress, or conform like everyone else, therefore you must be wrong."* Coincidentally, this is how I've felt as a follower of Jesus in a world of unbelief. Both involve a resistance to the fierce pressure to simply fit in.

In order to have some safety and peace, I just started hiding the BMX part of my life from others. I've actually talked to a lot of current pros who have the exact same story growing up. No one knew I was competing professionally by high school and that BMX had literally taken me around the world. It was really strange to not be fully known, but it was the price I was willing to pay to not lose myself. I wasn't going to give up on the sport that I loved just to fit in. Today I'm thankful for that rebellion. Having a discipline and sport to train at kept me out of a ton of trouble. More importantly, it kept me from compromising myself in order to look and think like everyone else. I guess my stubbornness paid off. Now I am involved with BMX at a veteran level; judging contests in the USA or Japan, and hosting the live TV coverage for some of the largest competitions around the world.

However for all the outward accomplishments I could point to, which hard work had earned for me, I knew I was constantly losing the contests on the *inside* of me. Things like being angry, jealous, negative or mean. There was a version of myself I wanted to be but I couldn't achieve it. Public victory is one thing, but it's private victory that we really want. I wanted peace on the inside that didn't involve hiding from anyone and wasn't motivated by impressing anyone. For all my rebellion there was still this gravity on the inside I couldn't overthrow.

IT TURNS OUT THE ONLY PERSON I COULDN'T REBEL AGAINST WAS MYSELF.

This is why I knew I needed God in my life. I just wasn't able to change the deepest parts of my life on my own. Pressure from others couldn't change me into who *they* wanted me to be. But I couldn't change myself into the person *I* really wanted to be.

It's the private victory no one sees which really leads to the public victory we want. But the private victory can seem impossible. Marriage was bringing my selfishness out into the spotlight. Difficult relationships started to pile up and I was feeling bitterness growing inside me. If you haven't experienced your own ugliness yet, just have a few kids. That's when the rage of my youth came back upstairs from the basement after twenty self-controlled years of keeping him medicated. The kids woke him up. No matter what your situation, we have all experienced the disappointment of being forced to face the imperfect person in the mirror.

I think the day that broke me was the day

my older son came home from kindergarten with his drawing of our family. From my psychology background I was actually pretty interested in it because the pictures kids draw tell you a lot about what's going on in their mind and how life is going. Is there a sun and smiles and all that? It means they are happy with life. Things like hands and fingers mean they are safe and have nothing to hide. No hands might mean they are ashamed of something. Well, I took one look at my son Aiden's picture of our family and my heart sank.

There was no sun. There were no smiles. There were huge blue drops coming down from our heads and black rocks flying out from our pockets. Not what I expected.

I asked him, *"Buddy, what's going on with our family?*

"We are all crying, Dad." He flatly replied.

That can't be good. Then I had to ask, *"What's with the rocks?"*

Without even looking at me he said, *"We are pooping, Dad. We are all crying so hard we are pooping."*

I said, "*This is not good."*

My wife was like, *"Thank you, Sigmund Freud!"*

As a dad this was not what I was hoping for. I didn't even look for hands. This was kindergarten code for SOS and it was the flare shot I needed. As I stared at this picture I began to wonder, *"How did we get here?"*

In reality our home was better than most, but my wife and I had started getting more frustrated at the boys, raising our voices at them and sometimes each other which we never really did before. It's something we had been able to control as singles and even navigate in our marriage, but the last year or so had gotten the best of us. My ugliness was spreading to others like a cancer. I knew change had to start with me.

I think we all have a bright sunny picture we want for our relationships, our friendships and even our own self-image. However every day we are faced with the reality of our brokenness, our temper, and the hurt we cause people around us – causing a big crappy mess. Some try positive self-talk, or something more spiritual like meditation to help. Others think they can just switch up spouses, leave their families, change jobs; but you take the real problem with you – *you*. The person I need to change is me, but I am also the problem. It's like trying to grab your own feet and lift yourself off the ground. You can't do it alone.

IF YOU WANT TO BECOME A BETTER VERSION OF YOU, YOU HAVE TO TAP INTO A POWER BIGGER THAN YOU.

Unfortunately, religious stuff hasn't lived up to its promises. And I will tell you right now religion is not the answer this book is pointing to. But Jesus offers a rebellion of a different kind and it's not what you think. His rebellion leads to real life.

My favorite call to action from the Bible puts it like this, *Don't just copy the people and opinions of this world or allow them to mold you into being like everyone else. Instead rebel against them all by transforming how you think on the inside. Be a unique and different person with a fresh newness in all you do and believe. Then you will learn from your own experience how God's ways will really satisfy you.*

That day holding my son's picture I was reminded that I needed God's help to change. I was faced with a choice to keep trying harder on my own, or reach out for something bigger than me. My wife and I asked God for help. Even though it didn't happen overnight, God changed our family. Jesus has helped me get back the picture I wanted, even with my failure. Almost a year later Aiden brought home another picture of our family. I was a little nervous to look, but when I did I saw this new picture had a big bright sun, teethy smiles, and even hands! We keep it framed as a reminder of the power of God to do what we couldn't do on our own.

I hope this book sparks a rebellion in you. A rebellion against being like everyone else who doubts God's relevance. A rebellion against giving up on the inner victory you desire. And a mutiny against the voice inside that says you can't change.

Chapter 2

LIFE IS NOT SHORT.

WRONG MOUNTAIN

When Bill Gates is giving away billions of dollars you need to pay attention. In fact, a few years ago Bill recruited some of his fellow billionaires (Mark Zuckerberg, Warren Buffet, and others) to do the same. They joined him in committing to give away over half of their wealth during their lifetime to philanthropies around the world. They call it the *Giving Pledge.* As someone who does *not* have a billion dollars to give away, I was intrigued. I started to google, "*How to start a philanthropy...*" but then I restrained myself. However, it made me curious as to where this deeper motivation was coming from. If happiness is found in things like cool cars, big homes, and stuff money can buy, why would anyone be giving it away so recklessly? Surely these guys are at the top of the success mountain, so they should be the happiest, most fulfilled people on the planet right? But now, if midway through life, they are giving money away – billions away – we should ask why? Where's the happiness in that?

"What does Bill know that we don't know?" I thought.

If I'm setting out to find happiness for myself, I should at least look to the man or woman on top of whatever mountain I'm thinking leads there and ask – is this the *right* mountain? In a way, Bill tossing away money to charity is a signal to the rest of us in the valley. He might as well put up a huge billboard at the top that says, *"What you're looking for is not here!"* And to drive the point home further, as of today Elon Musk, Michael Bloomberg and another 200 billionaires from 23 countries have joined the Giving Pledge. Giving away billions screams one big thing - rebellion against the empty promises of money and success. *It's the wrong mountain!*

Is anyone else feeling this way? Actually I see it everywhere now. Listen for it in your music. Singer, rapper, writer, and Pixar movie fan Jon

Bellion communicates something I think we have all experienced. He puts it into simple terms through his lyrics. Go find his song "*Stupid Deep*" if you want to hear it, but take a moment to read carefully what he says:

WHAT IF WHO I HOPED TO BE WAS ALWAYS ME?
AND THE LOVE I FOUGHT TO FEEL WAS ALWAYS FREE?
WHAT IF ALL THE THINGS I'VE DONE,
WERE JUST ATTEMPTS AT EARNING LOVE?
'CAUSE THE HOLE INSIDE MY HEART IS STUPID DEEP.

Just because the people I've mentioned have abandoned the *wrong* mountains, doesn't mean they are climbing the *true* one. Jon Bellion, Bill Gates, you, me, and everyone else is pursuing the same thing deep down. Whether you are Muslim or Hindu, atheist or spiritually connected, rich or poor, influencer or unknown, educated or illiterate, single or married, Western or Eastern, whether you lived thousands of years ago or you are the next generation – you have a hole in your heart that is stupid deep and this is why:

YOU WANT TO BE FULLY KNOWN AND YOU WANT TO BE FULLY LOVED.

But we haven't found both. There has always been a war inside us between those two things. I want to be loved but sometimes I am not that lovable. So in order to be loved, I hide the ugliness of my life. But this hiding means I can't be fully known. I deeply desire to be known but at the same time I'm afraid of the consequences. I fear, all the time, that I might not be accepted for the mess I really am, the true version of me. Have you ever had money, power, or influence but wondered if your friends really loved you – or even knew you? Have you ever been vulnerable and real with someone, only to have them ghost on you or not accept you for who you truly were?

Most of us are trapped in between those two desires; to be real or to be loved. We feel like we can have only so much of each, but never to the fullness we long for. We fear losing one over pursuit of the other. I would say most people settle for feeling loved but not known. Add to that the conditional-love of our world where you are only as good as your last performance. It's exhausting to be loved while feeling like you have to earn it.

Even in our own desire to be a decent human being, we can't really do it. So we settle for *looking like* a good person. Or looking successful, like we got it together. We know our hypocrisy within but we try to ignore it. So there we are, sort of trapped in a charade we have made. Guarded from being fully known because we fear we wouldn't be loved for who we really are. Our whole life might be spent searching for a place, a people, a community or a person where we can be both known and loved unconditionally for the imperfect mess we are. Sound familiar? I'm there with you and it's lonely.

Then there was this idea by C. S. Lewis. Lewis was a former atheist, disillusioned with the world, who later became the author of *The Chronicles of Narnia* books. He unleashed an idea I couldn't get away from:

"IF WE FIND OURSELVES WITH A DESIRE THAT NOTHING IN THIS WORLD CAN SATISFY, THE MOST PROBABLE EXPLANATION IS THAT WE WERE MADE FOR ANOTHER WORLD."

Made for another world? I enjoy the stuff in this world a lot, but does it *satisfy* me? That's not really a question I ask often, because there is always more stuff to get. New clothes, new gadgets, and new experiences could keep me busy (*and broke*) for a lifetime. But does it *fully* satisfy me? No. Not even close. Do I feel like I have enough of whatever I'm chasing? Never. They are crumbs of bread but not a real meal. This world might satisfy for a day, maybe, but the satisfaction doesn't last for long. Now that I think about it, I chase some pretty short-lived highs. Things as small as Instagram likes and followers to chasing recognition from people who are passing through our life for one act in the play and then never seen again.

Winning, by the way, is not enough to satisfy you either. Even Michael Phelps, with twenty-three freaking Olympic gold medals hanging around his neck ended up unsatisfied at one point. Because he had a heavier weight around his soul. Phelps actually turned to God for help, through a book from Pastor Rick Warren called *The Purpose-Driven Life.* Something about it helped him get unstuck when training and self-discipline were not enough. Many of the greatest achievers are actually chasing something really simple on the inside, usually approval from a person. You might be wishing for some final recognition, maybe a "well done," or "I'm proud of you" moment from your father that never came. Can I suggest that even *that* mountain is not big enough? You really need love from someone much bigger.

Another former atheist who found satisfying answers in the story of Jesus was author J.R.R Tolkien. One of the most powerful images, hidden within the story of *The Lord of the Rings* is the love story between *eternal* elves who had fallen in love with *mortal* men and women. Do you see the conflict? The elves are the ones with the problem. They have fallen in love with people that die. It's the perfect romantic tragedy, but it's still a tragedy.

You and I have the same problem on planet Earth. We fall in love with things that break, go out of style, wear out or die. Even if something or someone could provide fulfillment from birth to the day of our death, there seems to be something inside us that longs for even more? I think this is the *desire* that C.S. Lewis is talking about. It's stupid deep.

WHAT IF THE HOLE INSIDE YOU FEELS SO DEEP BECAUSE IT'S AN ETERNAL YOU.

What if the real you lasts forever? Then it would start to make sense why all of this stuff and the approval from all of these mere mortals is never really enough. You live in a world that is dreadfully temporary. People place all their desires and hopes in a job they lose, in a car that is remodeled each year, an iPhone that is redesigned every six months, or in a person that falls out of love. You out-last things all the time and it's unsettling. I think it is one reason why anxiety, depression, and suicide in our generation are through the roof. Nothing in this world satisfies. You and I could stand on top of the world and yell down, *"This whole planet is the wrong mountain!"*

Religion didn't satisfy either. Most tragic of all, people throughout history have pursued religious gymnastics that never feel completed. Maybe you tried church or religion and it didn't work. Or it didn't lead to a feeling of rest for your soul. That rest is out there, but it's not in religion the way you have known it. In the last century, millions of people from all around the world are rebelling against religion and leaving it for Jesus.

Author and former Hindu, now a follower of Jesus, Ravi Zacharias, explained his decision almost exactly the way C.S. Lewis did. Ravi said,

"NOTHING THAT LASTS FOR A SHORTER TIME THAN YOUR SOUL CAN TRULY SATISFY YOUR SOUL."

Let's ask this question instead: *What does God know that Bill Gates doesn't know?* This Jesus story from a few thousand years ago could actually be the real lasting thing you and I are looking for because we last forever. Being fully known and fully loved by an eternal God sounds like coming home to rest - eternally. On top of that, God has a purpose for your life in this world. The story of Jesus is more than just a religion choice; it's the fulfillment of a deep desire inside you already. You are chasing it right now.

I desperately needed the path that leads to Jesus because I needed everything he had to offer. But there was one big problem in the process. I had to figure out which Jesus was the *real* one and which were imitations.

Chapter 3

THAT IS NOT JESUS.

FREE RETURNS

If you asked one hundred people to explain the message of Christianity, the average answer would sound something like this: *"Just be a good person and you will go to heaven and all the bad people go to hell."* I would actually wager 100% would say that! And they would be 100% wrong.

The world is full of fakes. Fake news, fake watches, fake lips, fake hair, fake i.d.'s and fake degrees. I've almost lost trust in anyone. Most of us have experienced the gamble and frustration of buying stuff online. I've bought such legendary rip-offs as the "G-Shook" watch, as well as a zillion defective charging-cables. And once I bought these bike tubes made of some kind of Chinese rubber that smelled so bad – even after weeks of scrubbing – I finally had to throw them away. If you don't get the right brand, from the right source, you are probably getting the wrong junk.

So imagine with me that you bought a fake iPhone online from China, got it out of the box and (big surprise) it didn't work! The service didn't connect, the apps didn't run, and when you swiped up it sent all your contacts to Russia. You get the idea. To make it worse, imagine all of your friends had ordered the same fake iPhone too, because the marketing on it was that good. You would all throw them away (*and you should*).

Now this could lead you to assume that all Apple ® iPhones are junk. You might go further and resolve to never use *any* smart phone again in the future. But the real question is: did you make a *true* conclusion? If I'm the real Apple ®, I might hope that you reconsider by starting with the real thing.

Here is why we need to rethink what we have heard about Jesus too. What if we are wrong about the most basic message of Jesus' life to begin with? I've found his real message has become crowded out with imitations. And now almost 100%

get it wrong. This widespread idea of *"just be good enough and God will let you into to heaven"* is *not* taught in the Bible at all. Jesus *never* promised being good would get you into heaven, although people asked him what to do to get there all the time. I also found out it was the religious "good" people who actually killed Jesus because He said the *opposite* of this. Jesus actually bypassed the *good* people and welcomed the *bad* people, the rebels. We must start with the real Jesus before we choose to either dismiss him or follow him.

So which version of Jesus arrived at your door? Do you know what the Bible actually teaches about how a person becomes close to God? Did you get a counterfeit Jesus or did you get the real thing? Are you curious about the person all of history has been divided over? If I was Jesus, I would hope that intelligent people would reconsider and start from the beginning. Even if you are not religious, wouldn't you like to unlock a better version of you on the inside?

I know Christianity sounds like a weird myth and I'd be lying if I said I didn't struggle to believe it at times. But I want to tell you why I hang in there. I believe in Jesus because it's the real rebellion I need. Most of the loudest voices today in media, science, and education have developed an alternate story for you to believe in, one that rejects God as unnecessary and backward. To maintain a faith in God, many think, you would have to turn your brain off, right? However, the choice to *not* believe in a God actually takes faith too - lots of faith! I think our logic tell us there is something more behind how this world works. It takes courage to doubt your doubts.

WHO MADE THE STAIRS?

In 2019 I was invited to join sixty Olympic athletes for the second ever action sports event in Saudi Arabia. I was worried it would be a little sketchy but the people of the Middle East were super hospitable and kind. One day was set aside for a tour of the rare *Al Qarah Mountain* caves; one-hundred foot tall sandstone corridors, smoothed out by wind, leaving beautiful pathways through the mountains. To help more visitors enjoy these caves, stairs were built to make access easy, lights have been installed all throughout the cave, and handrails were added for safety. As the tour guide explained the thousands of years it took for the wind to smooth out this stone sanctuary, I began to mess with my friends.

"I wonder how long it took for the wind to make the stairs?" I joked. *"It must have been a few more million years for the wind to assemble those LED lights and the speaker system too."*

At least I thought it was funny. Of course no one was asking those questions, because logic tells you there was something – *someone* – behind the design of the stairs and lights. There was a creator, an architect with advanced technology beyond what could happen by chance. And it all had a clear, unified purpose to it. Now that I think about it, I wasn't worried if we would get out the other side of the caves either. You know why? Because a designer had brought us this far, I trusted that a designer would bring us safely home.

DOUBT YOUR DOUBTS

It actually shouldn't take rebellion to believe in God. It would take crazy faith to believe the lights and stairs inside those caves were created by a trillion years of wind. I believe in a creator God because I think it takes *more faith to not believe*. So for me it's actually not rebellion against logic. The only hurdle for many is the stigma of our culture, the same popular opinion that misjudged all my action sport friends growing up. That same media has told you the Jesus community is a bunch of hypocritical, anti-science, control freaks. There comes a time to start doubting your doubts about God. The narrative that we are a cosmic accident doesn't add up. God designed the universe with purpose and God designed you on purpose. You might have been an accident to your parents, but not to God. God planned your life.

My ultimate loyalty is not to a certain church or even an organized religion. I'm following a person, Jesus, who I believe is exactly who He claimed to be and proved it. Jesus claimed to be

God Himself, who came into the world in a miraculous way because of His love for us. God saw us and pursued a relationship with us. Jesus is fully God and at the same time fully man. While Jesus was on earth He was loved by the outcast and hated by the 1%. He spoke with divine authority, not with his opinions or to impress anyone. He performed miracles and raised people from the dead. He lived out a perfect life as far as his morality, his thoughts, actions, motives and his love. He caused an entire region of Rome and Jewish leaders, his own people, to either follow him or conspire to kill him. He was not politically correct, or passive, or a follower of any trend. Jesus was a rebel.

And being God, he was the first person to rebel against death itself and defeat it by *rising again from the dead* three days after being executed on a cross. History has had plenty of religious teachers and gurus, but this whole rising from the dead thing, as you can imagine, got some attention. It was the exclamation point at the end of his claim to be exactly who he said. Jesus proved true. And he proved it so well that thousands of years can't unravel His story.

If God designed you, and brought you this far, then maybe God has already engineered the path ahead. God has designed the world to work in perfect harmony for a bazillion years and He sees the eternal future. God sees where the story is going. So what if God has already designed a path to bring you into the life you've always wanted. So it's time to replace the fake Jesus. I'm going to give you a simple and perhaps completely new look at God. It's time to rebel against everything you have heard about Jesus, the Bible, the world religions, and even who you are.

Chapter 4

GOD IS NOT LIKE YOU.

SUPERNATURAL

My son Aiden used to keep a cardboard box filled with his most valuable findings, his *treasures*. Now "treasure" to a 7-year-old boy means a dozen bolts, bottle caps, bike parts, a broken radio antenna and an old chicken bone. I didn't have the heart to tell him his treasures actually had another name – *junk*. Some of the stuff in the box was probably even dangerous. His prize possession was his "scanner" that was a glued together hodgepodge of cardboard, a stick for an antenna, and a crayon-drawn screen with buttons. We pretended, of course, it talked with me when there was an emergency. Dad to the rescue!

That same year I was invited to speak to several thousand people about the way we form our view of God. I wanted to find a way to make the idea simple and memorable. After weeks of mulling it over, it all clicked for me one day while playing in the backyard – Aiden's box! So when my speaking event came, I got permission to re-create Aiden's box of treasures and brought it on stage. I had written on the side of the box "Super Natural."

"*This,*" I explained, "*is how most people have compiled their view of God and religion.*" Most people have patched together a view of God based on bits and pieces they have picked up in life from parents, a religious person, friends, movies, Joe Rogan podcasts, inspirational quotes, memes, or YouTube videos – it's "God-podge." Those one-liners about God have often come from unreliable sources, none of it actually fits together, and some of it is probably even dangerous. It's easy to get kooky views of God in our head. A.W. Tozer once wrote,

"WHAT COMES INTO OUR MINDS WHEN WE THINK ABOUT GOD IS THE MOST IMPORTANT THING ABOUT US."

Is God angry, or distant, or a force that's not like a person you consider relational or loving at all? Maybe you see God as the cosmic fun-killer, angry, uncaring, or an outdated and judgmental old man. Many people subconsciously put their biological father's face onto God, for better or worse. But the most upsetting thing is this: it doesn't work when they need it most. Maybe there was a time you used to believe in God, or pieced together something about God. Then you needed God to show up; an emergency, and it didn't work. For many people, it was a moment they were hurt. The wound led to anger at this creation they believed was god. When life was painful, God-podge was not super, it was not good, it was not powerful. So maybe you did the grown-up thing: You threw that whole "Super Natural" box away.

To be honest, I have a good enough imagination, and have heard enough stories of hurt and abuse, to put myself in that moment. So at this moment in my talk, fighting tears, I picked up my son's box, turned, and *hurled it* to the back of the stage. I watched bolts, bottle caps, bike parts and a chicken bone rattled across the stage, slamming into the back wall. The room was silent. I heard people gasp. I just threw away GOD! But this was just my point, *"What if, the thing that let you down, the thing you threw away, was never the real Jesus to begin with."* What if God didn't let you down, because that was never the real God in the first place? What you had was just religious scraps, or another name for it – junk.

I needed to find out for myself what God actually says about himself in the Bible. So during college, I decided I was going to rebel against all the junk I had heard and read through the entire Bible on my own. Who is God, and what is He like? I wanted to know what God says about His character and how He interacts with us. It took me over a year the first time through, and since then I've went back through the Bible every few years. I found the most reaffirmed attribute of God in the Bible was also the one most diminished in my view of God. God is not just good – **God is holy.**

HOLY ____!

Holy is like when you have something so special that you set it aside for a special occasion or attempt to keep it from being damaged. Rare baseball cards set in glass cases are treated as "separate." Priceless works of art are displayed in museums under high security, inaccessible to people and potential damage. Author Paul Tripp says, "*Our translation for holiness comes from the Hebrew word* qadowsh *which means "to cut." To be holy means to be cut off, or separate, from everything else. It means to be in a class of your own, distinct from anything that has ever existed or will ever exist.*"

Have you ever seen a penny lying on the ground and didn't even bother to pick it up? It's because a penny is not holy, separate or unique - it's common. Even though a penny is intended to have value, it has become so common we don't even consider it worth stooping to pick up. God is not common. God is the one and only God, creator of everything, eternal before all things, all-powerful, all-good in how he acts, and there are no other beings like Him. This is how the stories of the Bible progressively reveal our view of God as holy. But holy also carries the idea of pure and perfect in all God does.

Paul Tripp goes on to say, "Qadowsh *(holiness) means to be entirely morally pure, all the time and in every way possible. Everything God thinks, desires, speaks and does is utterly holy in every way. God is holy in every attribute and every action: He is holy in justice. He is holy in love. He is holy in mercy. He is holy in power. He is holy in wisdom. He is holy in patience. He is holy in anger. He is holy in grace. He is holy in faithfulness. He is holy in compassion."*

GOD IS 200% HOLY.

God is not a balance of good and evil. God is perfect in every way. God is both 100% absent of all that is evil and the 100% fullness of all that is good. He is 200% holy. We are not.

If you are familiar with archery, you have the perfect terminology. The distance from the bull's-eye to where an arrow lands is measure with a term called "*sin.*" You could win at archery by having a lower sin score than the person next to you, but perfection is not possible. Every archer has chalked up some measurement of sin, even in their best moments. Maybe more, maybe less, but the score is never zero.

When we lose the view of God as holy, we reduce Him to... *really, really* good. God is not just *good*; He is *holy*. The goal for us then is not to be *good* – it is to be *perfect*. If life was just about being better than Hitler or as good as Mr. Rogers, you might have a chance. But Mr. Rogers isn't our standard for what it means to be good, God is. And Hitler isn't our standard for what it means to sin, missing God's perfection is all sin. Sin is not only something we do that hurts someone, or when we break the laws, it is missing the mark of God's absolute perfection whether by millimeters or by miles. In that sense, we have all sinned. There is something about our sin that has broken our relationship with an all-holy God who is separated from all that isn't perfect.

In a lot of ways, we have tried to make the bull's-eye huge by comparing ourselves to other people or by making our own rules. This is exactly what religion tries to do. Jesus taught that religion, filled with rules we can achieve, is actually man's way of trying to make a bull's-eye we could hit. Ironically we still can't. I'll be honest; I can't even keep my own personal bull's-eye for myself. No amount of positive thinking and energy lasts for a lifetime. If you have ever made a New Year's resolution to have self-control in some area, you have felt the pull of sin to give in. Did you keep that resolution perfectly? Forever? Have you ever violated your own conscience in anger, deceit, or greed? If we can't keep our own standard, imagine how far off that makes us from God's standard? This is why the idea of being good to get into heaven or working off your karma with good deeds leads to one of two things: delusion or despair. You either have to lie to yourself about how good you are or face the reality that you have failed.

CHASING PERFECTION

I'll never forget being in Kobe, Japan in 2015, sitting alongside four other judges in what was the largest pro purse for any BMX Flatland contest I can recall. It was winner-take-all and first place would go home with $40,000. That's more than most of these guys with major sponsors made all year. At one point I remember thinking, *"Why did I even say yes to judging this? When today is over I'm going to have one guy that loves me and 99 people that hate me."* When it came down to the last two guys in a head-to-head final battle, the pressure was intense. The riding was so perfect and the level so difficult it was going to be a judging nightmare. Then everything changed. I watched the last rider lose his balance for half a second, come off the bike with only a dab of his foot to the floor, but the expression on his face said everything. He just lost $40,000. It was only a touch of the foot but there was no way to rewind it back.

At the capability and competitiveness of today's athletes, especially in action sports, one mistake in the beginning of your run and it's really over. A loss of balance and you are off the podium basically. It only takes one base hit and you are no longer pitching a perfect game. It only takes one loss and you are no longer undefeated. When you are talking about a flawless performance there is only 100%. Zero to ninety-nine are all in another category: not perfect.

Maybe you have watched the cringy-ness of an ice skater who falls on their first jump, then tries to finish their 3-minute performance with a smile. You know it, they know it – it's basically over. In fact, it's so mentally rattling they often fall apart the rest of their time. So when it comes to a lifetime of trying to keep God's holy standards, we have to be honest enough with ourselves to admit – it's over. Once we have sinned, there's no amount of cosmic community service that could erase it from our permanent record. There is no way that being good can roll back the mistakes and dirt we have brought into our lives.

Imagine you went into your local coffee shop and asked for an extra glass of water. But when they handed you the glass you notices something floating in it - a dead bug. Sort of ruins your day. Would you drink it? What if it was just a small bug? How much potential disease would you tolerate before you said, *"Nah, I can't drink that. It's not clean?"* Maybe that's a strange image but the water isn't pure. Of course, you and I wouldn't even want one speck of dirt in it. And technically even a speck of dust would make it less than holy.

Now this is where karma and religious rationale shouts its solution to the problem, *"Try harder to be good"* which is like saying, *"Just pour in more clean water!"* But does that actually make it pure again? Would a million gallons of good water, poured into that glass, somehow erase the fact that there's a particle of bug dirt? Nope. Never will. The only way it will become holy is to *remove* the dirt – all of it. 50% clean is not good enough for that water to be in relationship to your body again. 99.99% clean is not good enough.

And you, spiritually speaking, cannot be "good enough" to repair your relationship with a Holy God. No amount of good deeds, self-control, positive vibes, built up karma, or the charity of 10,000 reincarnated lives would remove the sin that we have in missing the mark of the holiness of God. This reality was terrible news once I was honest enough with myself to admit it was true.

How does Jesus feel about our sin? Not great. But Jesus wasn't looking for perfect people, he comes looking for honest people. Ironically it was the religious people who couldn't be honest about their sin problem. Jesus often turned up the heat on what it means to sin so they would get it. Jesus called people out for things like anger in their heart, lying, cheating and lusting after someone sexually. These are heart attitudes in which every human in history has missed the mark of perfection.

This is when I began to understand the uselessness of religion and trying to work my way to heaven by being good enough. The Bible painted a picture of God so perfect and holy it was ridiculous to believe any person could impress Him with our behavior, no matter how many good deeds. No one has had a perfect run in life.

IT'S POTENTIALLY TRUE THAT "GOOD PEOPLE GO TO HEAVEN," BUT THERE HAS JUST NEVER BEEN A GOOD PERSON.

When Jesus spoke, one thing became clear: being good was impossible. Jesus had to make a new way. His message was actually the opposite: that all people, good or bad, can be forgiven as they are. In the Bible we see a Jesus who is not disappointed, surprised, or angry at failure; but waiting for us to admit it. It was a group of prostitutes, fisherman, thieves, and misfits who found themselves friends with the God-Man Himself.

Jesus values what is happening on the

inside of us, the inner victory, not just outward religion. God isn't waiting to scold honest sinners, because Jesus didn't. Instead God wants to meet us in that very moment of tapping out and admitting, "*I can't.*"

CHRISTIANITY IS IMPOSSIBLE.

I like to win. I'm an achiever. Add to that being an American, which can lead to an annoying amount of over-confidence. And as an athlete I've learned to accomplish a lot of things I thought were impossible. Having mental self-confidence can actually account for some amazing triumphs. I've set goals to learn certain BMX tricks I thought were out of my reach, but eventually I got it. In my thirties, I set a goal to break a *Guinness World Record* in BMX because I thought it sounded fun. After seven years... and two failed attempts that we won't talk about because it's un-American... I did it! I got *two* certificates because I live in a two-story house and sometimes I'm that desperate for attention.

Being around Olympic-level athletes within action sports, I've seen the amazing potential of humans. They can learn almost anything they can imagine. After thirty years these sports are still progressing and people are still inventing *new* tricks. You would think we would have come to the threshold of what is possible but high-achievers and creative minds like this don't have a box or a ceiling that contains them for long. The action sports religion says: If you can think of it – with enough practice, willpower, and kinesio-tape – you can learn it. You can do anything... until you get hurt.

Unfortunately, I've seen the failure too. Getting injured is the first time many athletes have to face walking with a limp. It's the first time they have to have the humility to say, "*I can't.*" Maybe you have accomplished a lot in your life. Maybe on the outside you look like you live the dream and your social media is carefully curated to keep up that image. But deep down there is a private victory that is too big for you.

We all experience failure eventually. One day you will face the reality of being weak, or an emergency in life that is beyond your power, and you will need something outside of yourself. Maybe it will be physical weakness, like an injury, or maybe it will be moral failure. And when you finally *can't...* you will turn to something else. When we are most humbled, we often turn to God.

Take comfort, because the same Bible which makes God out to be impossibly good and mankind to be hopelessly broken, is the same place we find comfort of the great news; it's not up to us. The all-holy God never intended to place the burden of religion on mankind in the first place. Jesus flat out silenced the religious people with what He taught about God's love.

ALL THE THINGS YOU MIGHT THINK ARE WRONG WITH RELIGION, JESUS DECLARED AS WRONG.

What if you could discover a new view of God filled with what God says about Himself, and what he says about you? For that we need a reliable source to get our spiritual information from. Jesus has something to say about the God who created you and knows you better than you know yourself. He has not remained indifferent to your search for joy. God actually wrote to us in a book and He proved the message was from someone beyond this world.

Chapter 5

THE BIBLE IS NOT NORMAL.

PROVEN

Unnerving. That's the feeling I had as I saw Steve Swope flying around the corner through the parking lot on a used dirt bike. More terrifying was the fact that he was towing Mat Hoffman on a normal BMX bike at 30-35 miles an hour. This sounds like an old episode of *Jackass* that's about to go really wrong. If you have ever jumped a bike over a DIY plywood ramp in the front yard and crashed on your face in the grass, you might be picturing something like that. You don't know Mat Hoffman.

That day in Oklahoma City hundreds had gathered for one of the last grassroots contest events of the 90's. But Mat was on a side-mission to unveil for the world that he had engineered a way to go higher than anyone had imagined. Hoffman had built a ramp twice the size of a normal vert ramp. But to make it up the ramp took more speed than you could get by pedaling. Next logical solution? Have a dirt bike pull you like a ski boat! What could go wrong?

So I pushed my way to the front of the crowd lining up along what appeared to be a 200-yard makeshift pathway of scrap plywood. I barely had time to look up before I saw them coming around the corner. Roasting past me was Mat on his bike, wearing shorts and a full-face helmet, holding on to a ski-rope with one hand; as Steve was pulling him full throttle into action sports history. Steve veered off to the left of the target, and that's when I first grasped the scale of the twenty-foot high ramp they had made especially for this moment.

I think we all held our breath as the ramp sent Mat soaring straight up into the sky. The ramp was so large, Mat looked like he was in slow motion as he sent it a full 20 feet above the *top* of the ramp. And for a surreal moment the earth kind of stood still and Mat Hoffman floated over forty feet above the ground. When he landed a million years later the crowd of riders roared.

The photos, made famous by Brad McDonald, are iconic. Soon the story and the images of Mat in magazines and videos had made their way around the world. It was unquestionable – Mat was legendary. But was it just a legend?

WHAT CONVINCES US TO BELIEVE?

Before Photoshop, before deep-fake videos, there was really no question about if it was real. I guess someone someday could start a rumor that it was staged if they wanted. It would be a great conspiracy theory, I guess, that Mat and Steve made up this story and manufactured the images to become more famous. How would you prove it was true? You would find the eyewitnesses. They have no real motive to lie. And since there were several hundred of the top riders in the world there, it would be easy. In fact they are still alive to shut down any rumor to the contrary. There was actually an ESPN documentary called the *"Birth of Big Air"* recounting the details and witnesses of Mat's evolution into BMX greatness.

The action sports community is fiercely loyal to their patriarchs. If you posted this picture and started saying it's fake - you would get some swift and heated response. All kinds of people would come out of hiding to defend Mat. "*I was there*" would be the main defense. "*I was there and I know eighty people still alive who were there too.*" There are just too many eyewitnesses to disprove it. It would actually take more faith to believe all those people were collaborating around a lie.

WHAT IF I TOLD YOU THE STORY OF JESUS HAS MORE EVIDENCE THAN THE STORY OF HOFFMAN'S BIG AIR?

I remember picking up a Bible and the chapters were named after people, usually the men that wrote the book. Immediately I wondered why people didn't have more skepticism about it being "God's book." If men, who are not perfect at all wrote it, how did someone come to the conclusion that God was communicating to us through these sixty six books?

Then there was the content of the Bible to wrestle with. The book is full of hard-to-believe events, miracles, an unseen spiritual world of good and evil, and apocalyptic stories that describe the distant future. It was going to take rebellion against being like everyone else who assumed this was a fairy tale to give it a thoughtful chance. And an empty grave is the real smoking gun at the center of history. I would occasionally wonder if the followers of Jesus wanted Him to be their Messiah so badly, they simply embellished the life of a normal man, a good teacher, and back-filled the story with miracles to convince people to believe in their hero. Did Jesus really live, die, and then live again? If he did – I think I would listen to that guy! Can we be sure or am I just supposed to have blind faith?

Even if the Bible and stories that were passed down originally were inspired by God, throw in a few thousand years and how far off are the copies we have today? My college professor dismissed the Bible using a classroom exercise from childhood called the telephone game. She stated as a fact, "*The copy of the Bible we have today is unreliable, just like the telephone game where you whisper something around a circle and it comes out the other side completely wrong. Christians have been playing the telephone game with this book for thousands of years. There's no way it's close to the original. And it's full of errors."* I didn't know it at the time, but one modern discovery had proven this completely wrong.

WAS THE BIBLE ALTERED THROUGH HISTORY?

A lot is at stake if we don't have a reliable book about God and what He says about our souls. If God can't be trusted in what he says about the world and history we *can observe*, how can we believe Him in spiritual things we *can't observe*? I would have abandoned the Bible too unless there was a reason to believe we had something close to what the original witnesses saw and wrote. I've found that if you wanted to disprove the Bible, you are going to hate something called *archeology*. The Indiana Joneses of the world kept finding stuff that proved the Bible to be accurate. Archaeologist Nelson Glueck, former president of Jewish Theological Seminary and not a Christian, declared:

"IT MAY BE STATED CATEGORICALLY THAT NO ARCHAEOLOGICAL DISCOVERY HAS EVER CONTROVERTED A BIBLICAL REFERENCE."

And A. N. Sherwin, a Greek language expert and author, states that the confirmation of the Bible by our known history is overwhelming:

"IN THE GOSPEL OF LUKE AND THE BOOK OF ACTS, [THE AUTHOR] LUKE NAMES THIRTY-TWO COUNTRIES, FIFTY-FOUR CITIES, AND NINE ISLANDS WITHOUT ERROR. ANY ATTEMPT TO REJECT ITS BASIC HISTORICITY MUST NOW APPEAR ABSURD."

While atheist and skeptics like my professor ridiculed the Bible as having errors and being unreliable, scholars were constantly finding more credible and early portions of the books of the New Testament (the part about the life of Jesus and his resurrection). Stories which were circulating in writings as early as 80 A.D. Author and Greek scholar A. T. Robertson, summarizes what evidence there is for the Bible,

"WE HAVE 13,000 MANUSCRIPT COPIES OF PORTIONS OF THE NEW TESTAMENT. MANY OF THESE COPIES ARE DATED ONLY 80-400 YEARS AFTER THE ORIGINALS. BY COMPARISON: WE HAVE SEVEN COPIES OF PLATO'S WORKS, 1,200 YEARS AFTER THE ORIGINAL."

This means there were plenty of people still living who were around when Jesus died. Just like the eyewitnesses to Hoffman's twenty-foot air, they were there! The Bible states that at one point Jesus appeared to over five-hundred witnesses and taught them. So why is this a big deal? This appearance to five-hundred happened *after* he died on the cross.

This is why there are *no* writings from the same time period shutting down the resurrection claim as a big hoax. Because hundreds of people would have stepped in and said, *"It's true. I was there."* Eyewitnesses could verify, *"That story about him rising from the dead is not fiction, not made up, not invented – I was there!"*

CHRISTIANS DIDN'T HAVE TO PROVE THE RESURRECTION WAS TRUE. IT WAS THE OPPONENTS, ALL OF THE ROMAN EMPIRE, WHO HAD THE BURDEN OF TRYING TO PROVE IT WAS FALSE – AND THEY COULDN'T DO IT.

But there is one more thing that makes this book undeniably supernatural for me. The details of Jesus' unique life and dramatic death started, not *after* he died, but *before he was even born.* They were foretold. That's impossible for conspiracy theorists to pull off. And the predictions of his life were factually spot-on.

Prophecies about Jesus from the most ancient books, what's referred to as the Old Testament (written between 1200 and 165 B.C.), were extremely accurate. Imagine predicting things like Jesus' entire family lineage from David, the specific town of his birth, facts about his unique birth and his death. These details were too precise to be guessed by the thirty-plus different authors, who lived at completely different times in history, spoke different languages, and came from very diverse backgrounds. Books written in 600 B.C., like *Isaiah*, which contain dozens of prophecies about Jesus, seem so precise most scholars believed that details were altered later. Then something happened that was an a game changer.

The day this doubt about the Bible died was in 1947, when a Bedouin boy was looking through the caves near his home by the Dead Sea for a lost goat. Sound weird? Hang with me. He was tossing stones into large caves in the rock to see if he could scare out his goat from hiding, when he heard the shattering of clay pots. This would lead to the discovery of what are known as the "*Dead Sea Scrolls*." Preserved inside those shattered clay jars were leather scrolls, ancient copies of the Hebrew Scriptures, some dated at 100 years *before* Jesus.

Now remember the "telephone game" where copies of the Bible were passed down over a few thousand years? You would think books like Isaiah would be unrecognizable by now right? Plug in *Shakespeare* and give it a thousand years to be handed down and you would end up with the lyrics to *Despacito*. If my wife gives me a list of two things to get at the grocery store, I can't remember the second thing. So when the scrolls were found critics of the Bible and Christianity, like my college professor, were eager to see how corrupted the Bible had become and prove it all wrong.

In one jar, a well-preserved, entire copy of the book of *Isaiah* was found. They simply compared this pre-Jesus copy to the one we have today. What was the conclusion? Except for one or two spelling errors, they were identical. The telephone game argument didn't hold up. The critics were silenced. The accuracy of how Jewish leaders handled the meticulous copying of the Bible throughout history was found to be impeccable. One point for Jesus.

NOT ONLY DOES OUR COPY OF THE BIBLE PROVE TO BE ACCURATE, IT PROVES ITSELF TO BE TRUE.

If you were God, how would you prove that it's You behind the writing? You do something humans can't do: predict the future... perfectly. We are not talking about some fortune-cookie messages that are so vague they could be just as true of your *cat's* future as *yours*. Or some fortune-teller from *The Wizard of Oz* who is just a big fake behind the curtain. The Bible is not making vague, general guesses about Jesus being the foretold savior of the world. The Bible foretells such specific details about Jesus that only the Spirit of God, writing *through* normal men could do it.

Back to Mat Hoffman. Anyone could have made an educated guess in the 80's saying, *"Someday there will be a man who will go higher than anyone else in history on a BMX bike."* That's not how biblical prophecy sounds. So just for fun, I decided to write a parody of what the Bible prophecies about Jesus would sound like if they were foretold about Mat Hoffman instead. Enjoy.

A young man will be born un-expectantly to an unmarried girl during the month of January in Oklahoma City. You will call his name "Condor" because he will fly higher than any other BMX rider and he will save his BMX people from sports extinction. His father will come from a 2,000 year family tree of Hoffmans, specifically the Matthew line. Then during the month of September, two weekends after labor day, with friends standing on the deck of his ramp, their arms raised in victory; he will break records of extreme sports glory. He will go on to have 100 concussions, 14 surgeries, 50 broken bones, a 3 day coma, and then retire by skydiving quite a bit, painting, and performing crappy tattoos for friends.

THERE'S A MIRACLE ON YOUR BOOKSHELF.

The Isaiah Scroll is usually on display at the Israel Museum, but while it was touring North America, I actually traveled several hours, on the nerdiest road-trip ever, to see it with my own eyes. The prophecies about Jesus in Isaiah are so flawless that it would take way more faith to think men guessed it all, than believe God foretold it. The probability of even eight of those prophecies of Jesus coming true in one person was statistically considered impossible. And Isaiah is just the tip of the iceberg. The other books of the Old Testament contain over three-hundred more prophecies about his life. The Bible is not a normal book. It's a miracle on paper.

The Bible has basically closed the gap on the most popular arguments against it in history. The eyewitnesses would have been early enough to shut down any story that this was all fiction, and the prophecies about Jesus from writings in the past can't be dismissed in how they came true. There is no space left in the timeline for something made up by men.

THE BOOKS OF THE BIBLE, BEFORE AND AFTER JESUS, ARE A LITERARY X-MARKS-THE-SPOT ON GOD'S SON COMING INTO THE WORLD AS JESUS.

I can understand someone not embracing the *message* of the Bible, but math is stacked on the side of Jesus being exactly who the Bible claims Him to be. I don't get excited about arguing with people or trying to prove some book to be credible. It's what the Bible says about God's love-pursuit of you and me that really matters. God spoke. He spoke because He invites us to know Him. He didn't remain aloof at the brokenness of the world. He spoke through the Bible about the way back to Him and a new start. The reason you need to read the Bible is it speaks about this way back to God being completely backwards from every other way.

In the Bible, God never asks us to climb the mountain of religion back to Him. Instead God, in the person of Jesus, made a way by climbing down to rescue us. So what makes the message of Christianity rebellion against all worldviews today? It never elevates men and women to be their own savior. We are not the heroes.

Chapter 6

MAN IS NOT THE HERO.

YOU CAN'T MAKE THIS STUFF UP.

I've always been self-conscious about my name, *Claude*. It's not a normal name I know. It sounds like it could be a Bugs Bunny character or a French hockey player. When my wife Rebecca and I had kids, we started to think a lot about names and the meaning behind names. We picked up a couple of books one day to look up name meanings and did what everyone does first - we turned to our own names. My wife's name, Rebecca, is a beautiful name. It means *captivating*, *faithful* and all these noble qualities. So then we flip back to my name – Claude. As a man, you are sort of hoping for a tough meaning. Claude doesn't sound tough. So on my way to looking up Claude there was Mark which means *warlike hammer*; Tony meaning *praiseworthy*; Matt meaning *Gift of God*, and even Carl means *Strong One*. I'd settle for Carl. Rebecca was first to find it and her expression stiffened up a bit.

"Oh man, it's lame." she said.

"OK, just tell me. How bad is it?" I asked.

"No. It's Lame." She said, "Your name literally means lame. 'One who is lame, crippled, or walks with a limp.'"

You know, now that I think about it, no one ever asks me if that's my *real* name. If I meet someone named *Showtime* or *Princess* I always assume it's a nickname. I have one friend named *Fat Tony* and another who goes by *Catfish*. Surely, they picked that up somewhere and it just stuck as a pseudonym. But no one asks that about *Claude*. The *absurdity* of my name is proof that it's my *real* name. My parents must have done that because, let's be honest; no one would give themselves that name on purpose.

Another reason I choose to believe in Jesus

is that mankind would not invent a religion where they are the lame ones, where they can't do it. When mankind invents religion, you can tell because they all say you can be good enough – just try harder. Religion says: if you can follow our rules, if you can cease your desires, or if you worship this way, you will find peace. With enough practice and will power *you* can do it. In religion the hero is always predictable – us.

I BELIEVE THE MESSAGE OF THE BIBLE BECAUSE IT'S SIMPLY THE ONLY BELIEF SYSTEM IN THE WORLD WHERE YOU ARE NOT THE HERO OF YOUR OWN SALVATION.

We forever walk with a limp. As soon as you start to feel like you are back on your feet and it's up to you, you are back in religion. Christianity requires a rebellion of humility to admit we are spiritually bankrupt. In the financial world, there are two types of bankruptcy. One type is called Chapter 11 bankruptcy and the other is called Chapter 7. Chapter 11 bankruptcy is temporary. It's a time-out to pause, regroup, and get back on your feet financially in order to reopen for business at some point in the future. It's considered much less humiliating than having to declare Chapter 7. In Chapter 7, there's no coming back – you are done. In Chapter 7 bankruptcy you fold up the books, turn out the lights, and you bury it in the ground. There's no getting back on your feet, no regrouping around a new strategy or new leadership – you are finished.

THE DIFFERENCE BETWEEN JESUS AND THE RELIGIONS OF THE WORLD COMES DOWN TO WHO IS THE SAVIOR.

Religion might admit you have morality failures, or that you are not as good as your potential. There might be an enlightening moment to restart, change your life, and follow a new path. But they hand the reigns of redemption back to the wrong person – you. After getting back on your feet spiritually, every religion places the burden of salvation back on your performance. Religion makes you the savior.

MESSIAH COMPLEX

One pastor wrote his own little tongue-in-cheek story about a man who gets to the gates of heaven where he is told by St. Peter he needs a million points to get in.

The man responds, "*I've never heard that before, but I think I'll do alright. I was raised in a Christian home and I've never missed a church service. I went to a Christian school and have memorized the entire Bible. I'm an elder in my church. My children are all priests and missionaries working with the poor in India. I have always given over 30% of my income to charity. I'm a bank executive and work with the homeless in our city trying to get them low income housing.*

"How am I doing so far?" he asked.

"That's one point," Peter said. *"What else have you done?"*

"Lord, have mercy!" the man reacted.

To which Peter replied, *"That's all you needed to say. Welcome to heaven."*

Jesus rebelled against all norms because he declared something mankind was too proud to invent – that you and I were Chapter 7 bankrupt. We didn't need a quick regrouping and an inspirational locker-room message so we could go out and save the day ourselves. We need mercy and the humility to admit we can't.

WINNING BY LOSING

My good friend and pastor, Matt Brown, is an Iron Man athlete, surfer, and generally all things annoyingly-fit people do. A few years ago he was competing in a "Spartan Race." It sounds more like army boot camp, with mud crawls, wall climbs, and racing through a punishing obstacle course. One obstacle in particular was a tractor tire flip. Matt was one of the second or third guys to get to this obstacle. When he got closer he saw two guys bigger than him, each struggling to lift and flip these massive 6ft wide tractor tires and getting nowhere. So coming up to the tire, he reached under it, braced to lift it, gave one big surge and immediately let go. *"Nope."* He said, *"I'll take the penalty."* And off bounced my Iron Man pastor, humbled but honest about his inability.

Once Matt finished the race and saw his score time, he was surprised to see how high he had ranked. Apparently the other guys wouldn't admit they couldn't lift the tire and got stuck there wasting way too much time. Their pride wouldn't allow them to receive the time penalty as grace and move on.

But sometime during the race an official came over and discovered the problem. Each tractor tire was meant to be flipped by *two people* not one. What they were trying to do alone was impossible. But their self-reliance was their kryptonite. My friend Matt had the real inner strength, called humility. He had the wisdom to be real with himself, tap out and take the mercy penalty, and keep going instead of wasting time in self-effort.

The first step in following Jesus requires the same rebellion against our pride. Sometimes it takes the most strength to admit we need God's grace. Another unoriginal thing I hear a lot is that religion is a crutch. Christianity isn't a crutch, it's a crash cart. It skips right past wheelchair to the fact that you are incapable of lifting a finger in your own standard of being good. We are lame and it's time to call 911. Jesus didn't come to inspire people to try harder, he invites people to take the L and reach for His mercy. In the book of Romans in the Bible, the author Paul promises,

"EVERYONE WHO CALLS ON THE NAME OF THE LORD WILL BE SAVED." [ROMANS 10:13]

Everyone who taps out, everyone who has the humility to admit they can't, everyone who calls out 911 to God for mercy will be saved by Jesus. The idea that God gives us His grace free of charge is rebellion against our own ego and against our desire to earn it. But most of all this is rebellion that flies in the face of all the religions in the world.

Chapter 7

ALL RELIGIONS ARE NOT THE SAME.

TRIGGERED

Not everyone likes Christians. Sometimes I don't like Christians either when they come off offensive, arrogant, or as my Pastor calls them "Jerks for Jesus." However, I've also seen people get overly offended when Jesus is even mentioned. I've seen professors try to shame Christians out of their faith in a philosophy or science class. But I found myself the target of someone's frustration in the most unlikely place – at a parent's picnic for my son's basketball team. I was sitting across from a mom and having a normal conversation. She had graduated from an Ivy League school where I had visited before. Everything was pretty casual until she started asking what I do for a living and found out it had to do with Jesus. Then her entire tone changed.

"So you want to, like, convert people around the world to Christianity?" she kind of snarked at me.

As she got more aggressive about it, I noticed the other Christian parents at the table all got super quiet and tried to pretend like they weren't straining every muscle to listen. Now I'm not easily provoked by stuff, so I just kept telling her my non-profit helps people overseas, physically and spiritually. But she wasn't backing down. Subtly trying to hide how triggered she was, she actually took several more verbal swings at my faith to try to rattle me before I felt like it was fair to rattle back.

"*Yes.*" I finally replied, *"You know what? We* are *trying to love people and move them away from things like Hinduism because Hinduism doesn't help anyone. I've actually been to India, as well as several Hindu nations, and multiple Hindu Temples– have you?"*

"*No.*" she admitted.

"*Right,*" I leaned forward, "*Well karma teaches that you simply let people who are starving, poor, or hurting work off their past karma. That's why Hindus don't step in to help anyone in India.*"

I kept going, "*Have you ever studied Buddhism?*"

"*A little,*" she claimed.

"*Buddhism,*" I explained, "*Only helps others because the good karma circles back to your spiritual bank account. That's like saying a guy who buys a drink for an attractive girl at a bar is being 'generous.' Is he really though? Because ultimately the motive is selfish.*"

By now the other parents have stopped eating and are just staring, but I was hitting a stride.

"*Atheism that's worshipped at your Ivy League school is the worst of all. Because it teaches it's better to let the weak die. Hope you like the 'Hunger Games' because that's where naturalism leads.*" I wasn't done.

"*Christians however, have started 103 of the first 105 universities in America. It was Christians who fought to end slavery: motivated by the equal value God gives all people as creator of all. It was Christians who fought for equal rights and education for women: motivated by the value the Bible has always given women above the culture of the day. The Bible contains Christian women heroes, judges, leaders, deacons and it was women who were first to witness and believe the resurrection. The first Nobel Peace Prize in history was awarded to Henry Dunant, a Christian, for starting the Red Cross. Today, one-third of the world's hospitals are financed and operated by Christians. Because our core belief is not karma or the 'kill-or-be-killed' of naturalism. Christians are driven by the belief that God loves the world and sent His Son Jesus to die for the world, so that people could have life beyond this world. Show me something better!"*

Maybe that was too much, but I think I got tired of allowing people to be openly intolerant of Christians in the name of tolerance. Clarity is not bigotry. I was not trying to be unkind, but clear. God is both perfectly loving and loving enough to be perfectly clear about the reality of the world. When the stakes are life and death, clarity matters. You don't want your doctors to be nice – you want them to be clear. One thing God is undeniably clear about; there are not multiple paths, but only one true path to salvation and it's through faith in Jesus.

JESUS SAID TO HIM, "I AM THE WAY, AND THE TRUTH, AND THE LIFE. NO ONE COMES TO THE FATHER EXCEPT THROUGH ME." [JOHN 14:6]

On the surface, I can see how all the religions look similar. There are familiar wisdom sayings, guidance on loving others, and morality stories. So it sounds really arrogant for Christians to claim that their way is the only true way. That is arrogant *unless* there is something truly unique about Jesus among the other gods: unless He was telling the truth.

SEARCHING FOR TRUTH

One day I came home and my son was on his laptop, alone, and when I saw over his shoulder what was on the screen, I knew we were going to have to have a talk. You try to protect your kids from bullying, scary stuff, and violence, etc., but I had seen this disturbing content before. I didn't expect it to be included in his third grade homework, but hey, it's California.

He was reading a story about four blind men and an elephant, an allegory that's been repeated for decades to try to explain away truth. Now I was going to have to unravel this philosophical noose someone was trying to use to strangle his faith.

Let me tell you the story.

A king invites four blind men into his court to explain to him what object was in the room. The mystery object is an elephant, but as they begin to describe this creature they'd never seen before, each takes hold of a different part and a disagreement begins. "*It's a snake,*" says the man holding the tail. *"No, it's a banana leaf,"* says the man who grabs the ear. *"It's a sword,"* says the one who holds the tusk... you get the idea.

The point the story tries to make is that truth is relative; that all religions are the same deep down. What someone believes can be "*true for them.*" It sounds really nice, but it's actually absurd. Just believing it doesn't make a elephant an snake - it's still an elephant. The story itself has a bigger superiority problem – the narrating king. There is *someone* in the room that claims to have *all the truth* which us blind men can never have. The absolute truth it claims no one has comes from a narrator who is making a claim to have absolute truth. Tolerance can actually end up being equally arrogant, because it asks everyone to forfeit what they really believe.

ALL RELIGIONS ARE ALL WRONG.

Did you know that all religions disagree with the cliché *all religions are the same*? This isn't exclusively a Christianity thing. When you make a statement like "*all religions are basically the same, deep down...*" you really fail to honor *any* religion seriously. It would be the same as a white guy like me saying, *"You know, we are all really white people, deep down... on the inside."* Cringy yet? I hope so. It's just as absurd.

That's the same way a good Muslim reacts toward a Christian, Jew, or Hindu saying we all believe in the same divine being. And Buddhists are like, *"Bro, I don't even believe in a god!"* But there is, in fact, a central idea that other religions have in common.

THE ONLY THING THAT THE MAJOR RELIGIONS BESIDES CHRISTIANITY HAVE IN COMMON IS THEIR EFFORT TO MAKE THE ROAD TO SALVATION PAVED WITH YOUR EFFORT.

I've spent twenty years learning, reading, visiting temples, and talking with devotees of most major religions. Before we get to the difference in what Jesus taught, let me give you some quick insights in how religions all gravitate toward the idea of "being good." This metaphorical scale of good deeds and bad deeds is literally taught in Islam as the means to earn your way to heaven. Through the concept of karma and many reincarnations in Hinduism, you can evolve yourself into an enlightened being. And self-effort is also taught in Buddhism, where your goal is not to exist in happiness forever but to essentially disappear from existence forever.

I realize these are simplified descriptions but they boil down to mankind being the agent of salvation. All religions place the responsibility of salvation on the shoulders of people like us, who know deep down we can't do it. This is why many are spiritually seeking truth but at the same time resentful of organized religion. And I would be too.

EVEN THE CHURCH GOT IT TURNED AROUND.

Just as much as Jesus sparked an upheaval of religion, that same rebellion would keep the Christian message from being pulled back into the trap of religion in the future. The lure of keeping rules eventually crept in to what we call today the Catholic Church. They got turned around not because of what was actually *in* the Bible, but because most followers *couldn't read* the Bible in Latin. The Bible was never the problem, the lack of access to it was, and unfortunately a few bad leaders took advantage of this and began making up their own Chapter 11 rules again. Catholicism became Jesus *plus* something you do, and that was always wrong.

Have you ever wondered how Catholic churches financed all the beautiful stained-glass cathedrals across Europe? Unfortunately, they did it by literally selling forgiveness of sins for profit. Was that taught in the Bible? Nowhere. But did the common people have a Bible or speak Latin? Nope. At one point, Pope Leo the Tenth even admitted, "*The fable of Christ has been quite profitable to us!*"

However as the Bible was translated into a common language and the printing press made it accessible, people began to read for themselves and found that salvation couldn't be purchased by giving more money or by reciting more prayers to saints. True Christian faith is the grace of Jesus plus *nothing*. This wasn't some petty disagreement over opinions, this was clear from the Bible and it was cause for a rebellion. In 1517, Martin Luther would lead a *protest* asking the Catholic leadership to follow Jesus away from this manipulation of religion. The 16th century didn't have Yelp reviews so Martin did it the old-school way. Luther wrote his famous 95-point critique and literally nailed it to the front door of the Wittenberg Castle church for all to read. Even though he urged his friends to reform and change, they kept the new religion they had created. Those that left Catholicism in *protest* were dubbed the "*Protestants.*"

JESUS + NOTHING

I am a Protestant, not a Catholic because of what the Bible teaches. I hate writing this because it might sound like I'm picking on Catholics. I love my Catholic friends and there are some that still side with the Bible on this, despite what title they call themselves. In fact there are many Protestants today that have drifted away from Jesus back to their own effort. Whether you call yourself Christian, Catholic, Protestant, Mormon or whatever, the only thing the Bible teaches is that it's *never Jesus plus you.* True faith that saves is *Jesus plus nothing*.

I've discovered that most of my friends, who believe they have learned something about *Christianity,* actually encountered a version of *Catholicism*, still laced with religion. It's a counterfeit version of Jesus. In turn many friends have incorrectly assumed all religions are the same because a bumper sticker said it. Just like buying a fake iPhone and throwing it away – what many got by looking at Catholicism was faulty in the first place.

This movement called the *Protestant Reformation* was committed to one idea, which is the kryptonite to all other religions. The Latin phrase that united many Protestants together was the idea of *Sola Gratia.* It reminded them salvation is not through religion, or being good, or saying prayers, or confession to a priest, or communion at mass, but by something no man would have invented. Jesus plus nothing. In English it is simply "*Grace Alone.*"

The stories of the Bible *never* have mankind as the hero, climbing our way up the mountain. In the Bible, help always comes down to us from God. We do nothing to deserve it, because Jesus saves by grace alone. The song I mentioned by Jon Bellion has a second verse which tracks along with the same idea, as he wonders about a love that is more accessible than we think.

WHAT IF WHERE I'VE TRIED TO GO WAS ALWAYS HERE?
AND THE PATH I'VE TRIED TO CUT WAS ALWAYS CLEAR?
WHY HAS LIFE BECOME A PLAN,
TO PUT SOME MONEY IN MY HAND?
WHEN THE LOVE I REALLY NEED IS STUPID CHEAP.

The thing that might be most humbling about Christianity is how free it is. There are no pre-requisites or way of earning points with God. God is not in heaven yelling down at you to *"make Him proud!"* The love you really need is given stupid cheap. Salvation according to Jesus is *Sola Gratia*, by God's free grace alone. God's invitation in the Bible says it like this:

"COME, ALL YOU WHO ARE THIRSTY, COME TO THE WATERS; AND YOU WHO HAVE NO MONEY, COME, BUY AND EAT! COME, BUY WINE AND MILK WITHOUT MONEY AND WITHOUT COST." [ISAIAH 55:1]

THE HUMILITY OF RECEIVING

God wants to satisfy a thirst in you, if only you have the humility to come get it for free. There is something about religion and earning divine points that allows us to hold on to some pride, to maintain some of our self-reliance, and this turns out to be our core problem with Jesus. We don't have the meekness to let go and just receive 100% from God. Stupid cheap is too embarrassing. The world gravitates toward earning and Jesus knew this.

When it comes to the elephant of religion, Jesus says let go of it. Jesus also had a blind man illustration but his version goes like this...

"IGNORE [THE RELIGIOUS LEADERS]. THEY ARE BLIND GUIDES LEADING THE BLIND, AND IF ONE BLIND PERSON GUIDES ANOTHER, THEY WILL BOTH FALL INTO A PIT." [MATTHEW 15:14]

There *is* an elephant, Jesus warned, it's called religion. The only thing all religions have in common is sticking you with the bill of your salvation. They may all hold different parts of that ideology, but at the core they all put the work on your shoulders. That elephant, and the blind religions holding onto it, is named *self-sufficiency* and Jesus' antidote was to rebel against it before you follow it off a cliff.

The grace of Jesus is the answer the Bible offers to the problem of mankind. Grace lifts the oppression of being good off of you and puts it onto God's son Jesus. Rebellion against religion is actually the way home, to real rest and peace on the inside. Jesus Himself said it like this:

"ARE YOU TIRED? WORN OUT? BURNED OUT ON RELIGION? COME TO ME AND YOU WILL RECOVER YOUR LIFE. I'LL SHOW YOU HOW TO HAVE REAL REST AND TEACH YOU GRACE. I WON'T LAY ANYTHING HEAVY ON YOU. FOLLOW ME AND YOU WILL LEARN TO LIVE FREELY." [MATTHEW 11:28-30]

Can you imagine the freedom found in having a relationship with God like that? Can you imagine God as someone who fully knows you and He *also* chooses to love you anyway? Imagine God knowing all of your secrets and failures, but unconditionally inviting you into a friendship with

Himself.

The difficult thing about unconditional love is it's not based on someone deserving it. The most surprising kindness is when we give it away to enemies. When the big red justice button inside us says, "*Nuke them!*" – it's grace that says show them kindness instead. Unconditional love believes if there is a God, He can handle the justice in the universe so I don't have to. That kind of love bothers a lot of people though, because it doesn't seem fair. Giving "bad people" a second, third or tenth chance at forgiveness seems unfair. And that's just the point... God's grace is not about fairness at all.

CHAPTER 8

JESUS IS NOT FAIR.

THE GREAT EXCHANGE

I hate having car trouble. I hate it even more when it happens to my wife. After years of buying cheap vehicles, I decided to get my wife a really nice minivan. She loved it. Everything worked, it was reliable, the whole family was happy. Then within the first year, all of a sudden the van gauges began going crazy. It was overheating, making a horrible sound, and immediately we began to smell something burning. After towing it to a local shop, we found out that there was a crack in the engine. It was just a fluke problem, but it would need to be taken completely apart and I wasn't even sure if it could be repaired. The bottom line – it was going to cost an enormous amount of money and several weeks to repair. It was bad news.

Not only was the van possibly a total loss, now my wife had no way to get our kids to school. I felt like I had let our whole family down. The shop actually told me, *"You could just drive it until it dies."* I had one last hope for getting a second opinion, and perhaps by some miracle it wasn't as bad as they thought. In desperation, I reached out to a friend from our church community who owns a repair shop, to ask for his advice. Instead of advice, he told me to bring the van to him. He said, *"I want to fix your van and I want to do it for free."*

As I coasted our smoking van there, I was stunned and humbled. My mind raced for a possible way to pay him back or offer something in exchange, but I knew he wouldn't have taken it. It would have cheapened his gift to even offer. It was going to be free for us, but it would cost him a lot. So I had no choice but to just drop it off and thank him for the work and cost he was about to absorb for us. He assured me this is what he loves to do for people like us who serve our church. This is how God loves. But that wasn't the end of the conversation.

He asked, *"Aren't you guys going to need a vehicle for the next few weeks?"* He had just got back his Yukon, which had been loaned to another family, and offered it to us to drive until he got our van fixed. The next thing I know, I was handing him the keys to our broken mess of a van, and driving off in his huge beautiful Yukon. As I glided quietly home, my heart was just astonished at what had happened in the last hour. I went from 100% hopeless to 100% secure and I did nothing but ask. This man had taken care of all my needs, *Sola Gratia,* by grace alone.

THE DAY FAIRNESS DIED

Religion is really appealing if you are a hard worker and have a huge sense of justice. I struggled with Jesus at times because people didn't get what they deserve. I only felt that way when I still thought I was a *good* person. The more I realized how much I deserved the same judgment as others, the more thankful I became that God didn't dish out pure justice on me. Jesus did not treat us as we deserved.

You may or may not know the story of Jesus, who taught about God and stirred up such a rebellion that after three years the religious leaders were done with him. They arranged a sham trial with the Romans, unfairly condemned Jesus to death, and executed him in the cruelest way possible – being nailed alive to a wooden cross and hung outside the city alongside two criminals for all to see. Jesus was given a death sentence, but God had planned this exchange from the very beginning of time. Jesus' death on the cross was not really *his* death sentence – it was a substitute for *yours*. Jesus was telling the truth about His way to God being entirely different. It was entirely unfair. He was unjustly executed. We can be unjustly set free.

Remember the image of the cup of pure water and the speck of dirt? Jesus came to do what we could never do - clean the cup for good by paying for our sin debt. Our sin deserved an eternal death sentence to pay it off. This is why the Bible says *"the payment for sin is death."* It would have been fair for us to die an eternal punishment. But the great news is that God Himself decided to pay this ransom. When we say God's love is stupid cheap, that's not quite true – it was only cheap for *you*. It cost God everything.

"THE PAYMENT FOR SIN IS DEATH, BUT THE FREE GIFT OF GOD IS ETERNAL LIFE THROUGH CHRIST JESUS OUR LORD." [ROMANS 6:23]

Jesus' death on the cross took out the dirt of sin from our lives once and for all; He paid the debt, because according to the Bible the sin was placed on Him as a substitute for the justice we owed. It wasn't a fair trade. Jesus voluntarily received what we, in reality, deserved. This was truly the day fairness died. You can hand over your sin to Jesus and drive off inheriting his perfect life record.

GOD IS 200% HOLY, BUT WE CAN BE 200% SAVED.

So Jesus took care of problem number one: our debt. However we have another problem: our lack of goodness. Imagine are were not only a million evil-points in the *negative*, but we also need a million holiness-points to get in. In other religions you might find the idea of paying off sin. But even if a million reincarnations could atone for them all that would only erase your debt. It would bring you to zero basically. You also need a perfect life. You need another million points and the best you could give might get you to one. You won't find a solution in any worldview for how you can become 100% absent of evil *and* 100% credited with goodness. The Bible calls it being holy and up until now it was only a term used in the full sense of God. But Jesus changed that too.

JESUS CAN MAKE US HOLY.

Jesus lived a perfect, sinless life. And in the most unfair exchange of all, Jesus had the perfect run in life and he trades his life for yours. The Bible describes those who belong to Jesus as forgiven, clean, made new, reborn, his children, heirs, secure, friends, without shame, without fear, made pure, set free, and made holy.

THE WARRIOR AND HIS MIRACLE

One of my favorite stories from the Bible is the true account of a great warrior named Naaman. Naaman had everything he needed. He was loved by the king, respected and followed by his faithful soldiers, but he still had one horrible problem. Naaman had a skin disease called leprosy. Naaman's disease was highly contagious and would hinder him from being close to people, like his family. It would have even kept him from going into certain places of worship. He was *unclean*. Leprosy was incurable and he had no way to heal himself in his own strength. He needed a miracle.

Now Naaman had led raids as a cruel enemy of God's people, the Israelites. One day a young Israelite girl, who had been captured in these raids, was serving Naaman's wife. She was brave and compassionate enough to suggest that Naaman visit one of the prophets of Israel because God had the power to heal his leprosy. Naaman was desperate and humbled himself to go. He arrived at the home of the prophet with an entourage of horses and chariots. The prophet sent his messenger out with a promise from God to Naaman, but Naaman wasn't happy. Naaman felt disrespected that the prophet didn't even come to the door personally, but the instructions he sent were even more shameful. The prophet told Naaman to go bathe himself in the Jordan River, dipping into the waters seven times, and that afterward God would heal him.

Let me pause for a second to help you grasp why this was so appalling to Naaman. Back when I was in high-school I didn't have to worry about cyber-bullying, but I feared something called a *swirly*. Basically if you were in the wrong place at the wrong time, a small guy like me could be picked up by bullies, turned upside down, and your head stuck in the toilet while someone flushed it. Hopefully the person before you flushed. That was a swirly and it wasn't so much about the act; it was about the *shame* of everyone knowing what happened. In ancient near east, hygiene was a big deal. It could bring shame on you and your entire family by simply touching a dead animal or dead body. And there were no antibiotics; if you got in the wrong situation it could kill you.

This Jordan River that Naaman was being sent to was downhill and downstream from all the populated cities which means it gathered all of the waste that flowed down. In a world before plumbing, it was one of the filthiest rivers in the region and you can imagine the smell. It was the sewer line of Israel. The humility and foolishness of choosing to dunk yourself in it was unbearable for

Naaman.

Naaman was outraged. Was this a trick because he was an enemy of Israel? Give myself a swirly in the Jordan River? This was the opposite of what he was imagining. He had hoped the prophet would give him a great noble task to complete, or wave his hands in the air to his god, say an enchantment, and some elaborate miracle would take place. That would be a much better story to tell for such a noble warrior. However Naaman's servant finally spoke wisdom into the situation. He reasoned with Naaman to get beyond his own pride saying,

"If the prophet had told you to go and do something very difficult, wouldn't you have done it? So you should certainly obey him when he says simply, 'Go and wash and be cured!"

Naaman had to choose between doing something that looked "religious" or trusting God enough to put his faith in something simple and foolish. He had to rebel against the strongest enemy he had ever faced, his own pride.

"So Naaman went down to the Jordan River and dipped himself seven times, as the man of God had instructed him. And his skin became as healthy as the skin of a young child, and he was healed!'"

Naaman was healed through believing God's promise – that's it. The miracle was free and easy;

it only cost him the humility to accept it. But that doesn't stop Naaman from the next logical religious thought – maybe I can *pay God back.*

"Then Naaman and his entire party went back to find the man of God. They stood before him, and Naaman said, 'Now I know that there is no God in all the world except in Israel. So please accept a gift from your servant.'"

But the prophet knows God's unconditional love cannot be bought with good works, with gifts, with karma, with our self-effort or earning. So the prophet refuses to let Naaman pay it back and replies,

"As surely as the Lord lives, whom I serve, I will not accept any gifts."

Naaman actually doesn't get what he deserves. He was not a nice guy and didn't do a bunch of nice things. He didn't turn his life around like Scrooge before he was healed. In a lot of ways the justice seems to be missing. Naaman did nothing but believe the promise of God.

THE WORK OF BELIEF

The world today believes a lot like Naaman did. We live in a culture where love is often transactional. You give me *this* and I will give you *that*. If you do your part, I will do my part. The world's affection can be gained over a lifetime and lost in one tweet. Religion assumes God is the same, conditionally-loving dad on the sidelines yelling at his son, *"Go make me proud!"* I've never liked that phrase. As if the world operated in some kind of emotional Hunger Games.

God gives you a new life, forgiven and free. You can't even pay it back. But just like Naaman, it takes rebellion. We must rebel against our pride to walk into those waters in a world that says nothing is free. Every time someone asked Jesus what to do to get into heaven, it reminds me of Naaman coming to the prophet asking for a miracle. Jesus didn't give impressive religious answers either, but something simple and humbling.

THEN THEY ASKED JESUS, "WHAT MUST WE DO TO DO THE WORKS GOD REQUIRES?" JESUS TOLD THEM, "THIS IS THE ONLY WORK GOD WANTS FROM YOU: BELIEVE IN ME." [JOHN 6:28-29]

And this is Jesus' only answer; *believe* in what He has done for you. Even for harsh enemies like Naaman, Jesus says believe that imperfect people like you and I can be forgiven by God.

No matter what your story is or your past, you can experience the same love and acceptance by God. I've seen God heal thousands of broken marriages and families. I've seen Jesus soften hearts what were hardened by pride, anger and hurt. I've see God give courage to timid men and women who became unlikely leaders. I've seen him pour out generosity through an entire community of people, all of whom were set free the way I had been. And Jesus can change you if you ask him. God gives us an awesome new life not by religion, but by grace. Grace says you don't deserve it or earn it; you can only receive it. Jesus says our only work is to believe.

Mankind, just like Naaman, had an overwhelming problem and needed a miracle. God did not turn us away but came running into the fire. Some people wonder where God is in the middle of all the painful things that happen in our world. Does God care? Is He not powerful enough to stop evil? If Jesus already met our greatest need in the big story of history, maybe God has a plan to bring about a good ending to your story too.

Chapter 9

THE STORY IS NOT OVER.

PLOT TWIST

I love stories with a plot twist. The best stories are the ones with a surprise at the end that leaves everything resolved. We get pulled in because we seek resolution. It's one of the reasons you have sat down to watch one episode of something on Netflix and next thing you know, it's been three days of binge watching, you have eaten an entire cake, and lost your job. We want all the tension to resolve somehow in the end, but until we can see the end it leaves us restless. We don't like the tension of being mid-story.

There have been so many times in my life that I have wondered why I am going through something painful. Or heard news of the latest tragedy, suicide, school shooting, environmental destruction, political cover-up, or friend with cancer and asked *why*? Why God? I can't see any way out of this tension, any purpose in this pain, any goodness of God in the suffering of man. Is God on vacation? Is God not strong enough to stop the middle-schooler with a gun? Is God not loving enough to just zap the planet with some radiation waves and hit reset on all the cancer at once? Pain is a problem for my faith, but it's not proof against God. In fact, evil proves that something is inherently broken about the world and we know it deep down.

I remember my dad taking me to the best movie that has ever been made, *The Empire Strikes Back*. I was five years old and it was my first time to see a movie on the premier weekend. Two hours later I was a little stunned. Luke lost a hand, kissed his sister and found out his real dad was the most evil person in the universe. That story sounds more like a dysfunctional family reunion on the 4th of July than the Star Wars story I was expecting. The good guys didn't win in the end. Han Solo was a wall decoration and Boba Fett got away. What the heck? I had to wait *five more years* for the rest of the story. That was half of my entire life living with tension unresolved! There was a good end coming, I just couldn't see it yet. But when you look back at the entire saga you see: it was all for the best in the end. The dark side loses. The rebels win.

OUR PROBLEM WITH PAIN IS THAT LIFE IS NOT RESOLVED IN TWO HOURS LIKE A ROMANTIC COMEDY.

The Bible is actually not shy about the fact that evil has been brought into the world and that people are touched at times by pain. We were the ones that brought sin and the effects of sin into the world, not God. There are some tragedies that we just don't understand but most things are tied to consequences of doing things our way instead of God's way. Han Solo was a shady smuggler who got caught. Princess Leia was trying to make Solo jealous. And Luke didn't listen to Yoda and finish his training. We get angry at God for not bailing us out of every bad decision He warned us not to do in the first place. The world is broken and we broke it. But do you believe God is a better author than George Lucas or J.J. Abrams? If those guys can write a plot twist that leaves you in tears, exclaiming "*It was all for good,*" why is it hard to believe God can do even better?

IF EVIL APPEARS POINTLESS TO ME, THAT DOESN'T MAKE IT POINTLESS.

The Bible is full of stories of evil that were flipped for good. The stories of normal people who follow God are there to give us hope that God can bring us through the fire. I've learned the greatest lessons in life, not during times of ease, but during times of difficulty. You can't see the end. When I can't even see the plot twist of a two hour movie, why would I expect to make a final judgment call about the purpose of evil in a story that spans all of history? It's a story that's not even over yet.

THE PERSPECTIVE OF A 100-YEAR LIFE CANNOT SEE THE PURPOSE OF AN ETERNAL STORY.

The clearest example of God flipping evil for good is in the death and resurrection of His Son Jesus Christ. Don't let anyone say that God is distant or unconcerned with evil. God was not only grieved by the suffering of this world, He entered into the evil Himself to do something about it once and for all. In the greatest plot twist in history, God put *Himself* on the hook for the sin of our world. God was perfectly good in sending His Son and perfectly powerful in bringing Jesus back from the dead. If God allowed Jesus to suffer and die, it wasn't because He didn't love him – it was because He had a bigger plan for good. And God has a plan for good in your life too.

"IN THIS WORLD YOU WILL HAVE TROUBLE. BUT TAKE HEART! I HAVE OVERCOME THE WORLD." [JOHN 16:33]

The cross did not have the last word over the story of Jesus and evil will not have the last word in the story of you. You can have 100% assurance that the end of your story will be for good.

ARE YOU ZERO OR ONE-HUNDRED?

Once a friend asked me if I thought I would go to heaven after I died. I didn't know for sure and it sounded arrogant to say *yes* so I answered, *"I think I'm like 75% sure."*

He laughed.

"You mean zero?" he replied. *"The only options are zero and one-hundred percent."*

I wasn't tracking with him yet.

People who are trusting in themselves are never 100% sure about what's going to happen when they die. Because if it's up to us, we know we are not perfect, not even 90% perfect. The Bible says there is a way to be 100% sure, but only when it's *not* dependent on us. My friend showed me a verse in the Bible where the author John makes the math really simple,

"WHOEVER HAS THE SON HAS LIFE: WHOEVER DOES NOT HAVE THE SON OF GOD DOES NOT HAVE LIFE." [1 JOHN 5:12]

If you believe in Jesus, the Son, you can be 100% sure about where you stand with God right now. It's 100% because it's up to Jesus, the only perfect person, and not based on your performance. When I said I was 75% sure I'm not even sure where I got that number. I just pulled it out of my head. Was I basing that on everyone else I knew or my own standards? What number would you give yourself? What I unintentionally revealed in my 75% is that deep down I was still trusting in my effort. And 75% or even 99% really means I am not really trusting in the Son of God. And according to John, if we don't have the Son of God we don't have life. My friend was right; it's either zero or one-hundred.

ZERO ASSURANCE.

Some of the most famous people who lived their entire lives with confidence that there was no God, nothing beyond the grave, and no need to pursue a spiritual life, came to their deathbed with less assurance about their ideas. Listen to what has been told of their last words.

"I am abandoned by God and man; I will give you half of what I am worth if you will give me six months' life."
Voltaire

"O God, if there be a God, save my soul, if I have a soul!"
Robert Ingersoll

"I am in flames!"
David Hume

"My philosophy leaves me utterly forlorn!"
David Strauss

"Now it is nothing but torture and makes no sense anymore."
Sigmund Freud

"O Lord, help me! Christ, help me! No, don't leave; stay with me! Send even a child to stay with me; for I am on the edge of Hell here alone."
Thomas Paine

"Until this moment, I thought there was neither God nor hell; now I know and feel that there are both, and I am doomed by the just judgment of God!"
Sir Thomas Scott

"All my possessions but for a moment of time!"
Queen Elizabeth
"I say again, if I had the whole world at my disposal, I would give it to live one day. I am about to take a leap into the dark."
Thomas Hobbs

"For the first time in fifty years I find myself in the slough of desperation... All about me is darkness, I am praying for light."
Gandhi

"All of the wisdom of this world is but a tiny raft upon which we must set sail when we leave this earth. If only there was a firmer foundation upon which to sail, perhaps some divine word."
Socrates

ZERO FEAR.

However, listen to the last words of famous Christians; people who rebelled against doubts, against the mocking of others, who endured danger and threats to their life for their faith. These rebels were authors and pastors – names you may not recognize but they knew Jesus and trusted him in life. And the tone in their voice gives us a hint that they were entering into the next reality with certainty and without fear.

"Trust in God and you shall have nothing to fear."
Jonathan Edwards

"I am going to Him whom my soul loves, or rather who has loved me with an everlasting love, which is the sole ground of all my consolation."
John Owen

"My dear children do not grieve for me. I am my God's. I belong to Him. I go but I trust to meet you all in heaven."
Andrew Jackson

"I see earth receding; heaven is opening. God is calling me."
D. L. Moody

"I commend my soul into the hands of God my Creator, assuredly believing, through the only merits of Jesus Christ my Savior, to be made partaker of life everlasting."
William Shakespeare

"Into Thy hands I commend my spirit! You have redeemed me, O God of truth."
Martin Luther

"This is the last of earth. I am content!"
John Quincy Adams

"I am going home."
David Livingstone

I AM GOING HOME.

The Bible says if we have this kind of relationship with God we can be 100% sure that God is working all things in our story for good. We can live life with hope in the face of a broken world. We can be free from anxiety and fear in confidence of a God who can even raise people from the dead. God can raise your story from the grave no matter what you have done. God has never turned a blind eye from the pain and evil in this world. In fact he ran into the fire for you, letting His Son Jesus absorb the heat of it all in His death. This was the ultimate plot twist in all of history.

Love makes a way when there seems to be none. That's the theme of the last chapter, the story of Michel the Japanese goldfish.

Chapter 10

THE SALVATION OF MICHEL THE GOLDFISH.

FRIENDSHIP

One of my good friends and favorite people to follow on social media is Matthias Dandois from Paris. He is an incredibly likeable BMX champion, Redbull athlete, fashion model, movie star, and global traveler who is constantly on the go. Last year he traveled 263 days to 15 countries, often getting tattoo souvenirs at each stop, which cover much of his upper-body. My boys love him and every time I take a trip to a contest they ask, *"Are you going to see Matthias?"*

On a recent trip to Japan, Matthias decided to add some extra excitement and purchased a buddy – a goldfish which he named Michel (*pronounced with a French accent, Michelle*)

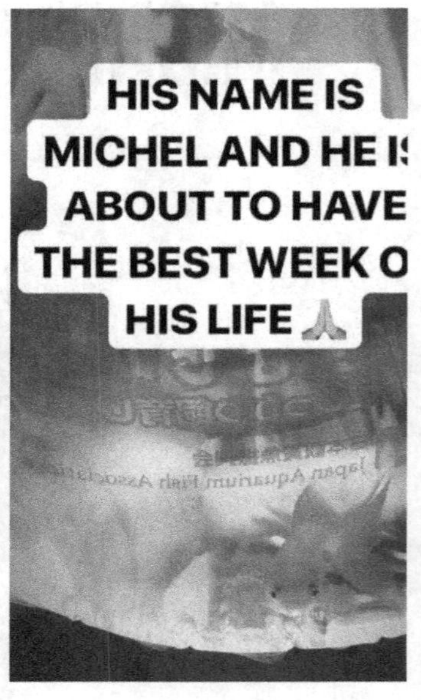

Michel rode along for some hilarious adventures from facing his fears of sushi restaurants and cat posters, being checked in at the coat check at an opera, living the high life in a five star hotel bathtub, and appreciating Japanese art museums. Now that I think about it, Michel had a better week with Matthias than most people have all year.

MICHEL FACING HIS
DEEPEST FEARS

MORNING CRUISE WITH
MICHEL

"CAN I HAVE
MY GOLDFISH
BACK PLEASE?"

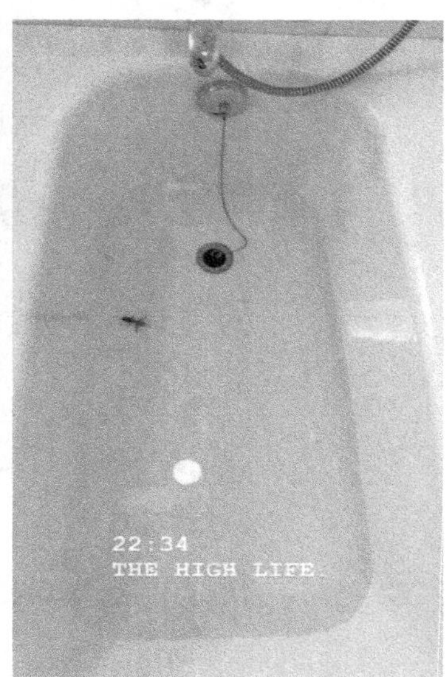
22:34
THE HIGH LIFE.

But my friend Matthias broke rule number one. Never bond with a goldfish. Michel had grown on him and now Matthias had a problem – he couldn't bring Michel home. So toward the end of the week Matthias started tweeting at Air France.

"Hey @AirFrance, is it possible to bring a small goldfish back to France from Japan? This is really important. Merci."

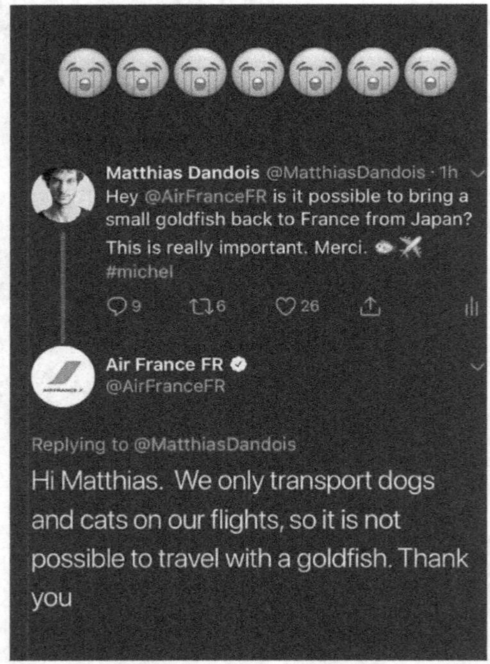

But the answer was no. The internet, however, did not let go without a fight.

FINDING A WAY HOME.

Almost immediately thousands of mutual friends and followers began offering the most creative solutions I have ever heard. It was hilarious. It was rebellion against all odds. *We are high performance athletes! We can find a way!* Entire threads blew up around the repurposing of an 8oz bottle. Discussions began around the probability of surviving a check-in bag and airline cargo temperatures. I learned a lot.

One person even suggested that Matthias toss Michel inside his mouth during the TSA screening and hope they don't ask him any questions until he passes through. Air France was not going to have the last word!

But plan after plan made it clear: there was no way, realistically or legally, for Michel to pass through to the other side without dying in the process. Goldfish are too fragile. The TSA security is too tight. It was impossible. The adventures of Michel the Goldfish and Matthias Dandois would have to come to an end.

So on the last day, I noticed that Matthias had posted another story. By now I was emotionally drawn into this stupid saga and I remember being a little anxious as I waited for my phone to load.

His last post was letting everyone know that he had given Michel to the young son of another Japanese friend to care for. However, there was a *"But..."* The next post simply read, *"Michel will be with me for the rest of my days..."*

The morning before leaving, he had an image of Michel the goldfish tattooed on the back of his hand. In all this, I saw something beautiful and filled with truth so I immediately messaged him.

My text to Matthias simply said this. *"Friend, this is how God feels about you."*

GOD SAYS IN ISAIAH, "I WILL NOT FORGET YOU. BEHOLD, I HAVE ENGRAVED YOU ON THE PALMS OF MY HANDS." [ISAIAH 49:15-16]

God is not distant from this world. He sees you. He has bonded with you more than you think, and he invites you to be forever secure in your relationship with him. If you can't do anything to earn it, you can also be assured you can't do anything to lose it.

MICHEL THE GOLDFISH NEVER MADE IT HOME. BUT YOU CAN.

One-hundred trillion human minds or plans could never come up with a way to save you, but God did. Religion couldn't do it, because it required someone passing through death. Someone who could also bring us back to life on the other side. The resurrection of Jesus was the proof that God accepted his payment for sin. Jesus did it, he defeated death. Jesus passed through to the other side and can raise us to life on the other side. God not only remembers you, but God created a way to bring you home. This is what it means to be saved.

You and I don't have to wait until we are on the TSA belt of our own deathbed to find out what we really believe deep down. Chances are you already know where you stand with Jesus. You know if you are holding on to your own way, trusting in some inner strength to power through life to maybe impress God – if there is a God? Maybe you are ready to rebel against doubt and against what everyone else says to make a choice of your own. What if the life you are seeking is as close as a simple, genuine prayer to Jesus.

THE PATH YOU WERE MADE FOR WAS MADE ONLY FOR THE REBELS.

If you want to be different, choose to follow Jesus. He actually describes his way as the cosmic minority way. It was never going to be mainstream, or cool, or popular, or easy, but it is truth.

"FOR WIDE IS THE GATE AND BROAD IS THE ROAD THAT LEADS TO DESTRUCTION, AND MANY ENTER THROUGH IT. BUT SMALL IS THE GATE AND NARROW THE ROAD THAT LEADS TO LIFE, AND ONLY A FEW FIND IT." [MATTHEW 7:13-14]

FINDING THE NARROW PATH OF GOD.

This might be the spark that ignites something inside you to pursue more. Don't give up. Don't come this far and then try to turn off the voice inside you that is inviting you to seek God. That voice is God. You can actually hear from God directly in a much better book, the Bible. If you don't own a Bible there is a free Bible app called YouVersion that will help you get started.

If someone gave you this book as a gift, circle back with them and let them know your questions. Ask them how they decided to follow Jesus.

Depending on where you live, there might be a church that believes people are saved by the grace of Jesus alone. Ask those questions of someone to see if that might be a good faith community for you to discover more about Jesus. Start meeting other Christians who genuinely follow God. One of the greatest joys of following Christ is finding a loving family of others, where you can be known and loved the way God intended. If you don't have a church you can find a great online community at the church I sometimes teach at called *Sandals Church*. It's all free online at www.sandalschurch.com.

Lastly, you can't find the path until you are ready to rebel against trusting in yourself and simply call out to Jesus. You don't need a priest or fancy words; you can believe and join God's family right now. God actually saw this very moment from eternity past. He saw you holding this book. Even now He sees and hears you. God himself planned to bring you to the brink of a moment where you would crash into Him and a path would open up in front of you. There is a wide path behind you; you already know that one and what it offers. The majority of people will never leave that wide path, but you can. Because I believe inside you there is a rebel too.

My prayer is that you would ignite that same courage which has always made you unique, counter-cultural, and creative; to step bravely into a new allegiance to Jesus, the Christ, the Savior of the world. God designed this moment. It's your moment to rebel.

BOOKS THAT HAVE HELPED ME EXPLORE FAITH IN JESUS:

MORE TOUGH QUESTIONS?

Tim Keller, *The Reason for God*

Lee Strobel, *The Case for Christ*

C.S. Lewis, *Mere Christianity*

Ravi Zacharias, *Jesus Among Other Gods*

HOW DO I LIVE LIKE JESUS?

Henry Blackaby, *Experiencing God*

A. W. Tozer, *The Pursuit of God*

Jerry Bridges, *Transforming Grace*

John Piper, *Desiring God*

ENDNOTES

Pg. 16 | *"Stupid Deep,"* Glory Sound Prep by Jon Bellion, Visionary Media Group and Capital Records, released Nov 2, 2018.

Pg.18 | "If I find in myself a desire which no experience in this world can satisfy, the most probable explanation is that I was made for another world." (C.S. Lewis, *Mere Christianity, Bk. III, chap. 10, "Hope")*

Pg.21 | "Nothing that lasts for a shorter time than your soul can truly satisfy your soul." (Ravi Zacharias, *Jesus among other gods, Thomas Nelson, 2000)*

Pg. 31 | "What comes into our minds when we think about God is the most important thing about us." (A.W. Tozer, *The Knowledge of the Holy, New York: HarperCollins, 1978), 1.*

Pg. 33,34 | *Paul Tripp defines the holiness of God. https://www.paultripp.com/articles/posts/the-doctrine-of-holiness-article*

Pg. 49 & 50 | Various Scholars weigh in on the credibility and historic evidence of the Bible. You can find those sources and more here: https://probe.org/the-new-testament-can-i-trust-it and https://probe.org/category/reasons-to-believe/reliability-of-the-bible

Pg. 61 | Tullian Tchividjian story adapted from an article, http://theresurgence.com/2011/11/29/you-must-have-1-000-points-to-enter-heaven accessed 11/29/11 no longer available.

Pg. 74 Pope Leo tenth | https://en.wikiquote.org/wiki/Pope_Leo_X And another great summary of the Protestant Reformation can be found here: https://zondervanacademic.com/blog/how-the-protestant-reformation-started

Pg. 85 The Story of Naaman can be found in the Bible, the book of 2 Kings chapter 5.

Pg 100 The Story of Michel the Goldfish used by permission of my friend Matthias Dandois. @matthiasdandois

CPSIA information can be obtained
at www.ICGtesting.com
Printed in the USA
LVHW080814260220
648116LV00006BA/1030

9 780578 645643